PRIMARY SOURCES IN AMERICAN HISTORY™

Manifest Destiny

A Primary Source History of America's Territorial Expansion in the 19th Century

J. T. Moriarty

The Rosen Publishing Group, Inc., New York

Published in 2005 by The Rosen Publishing Group, Inc.
29 East 21st Street, New York, NY 10010

Library of Congress Cataloging-in-Publication Data

Moriarty, J. T.
Manifest destiny: a primary source history of America's territorial expansion in
the 19th century/by J. T. Moriarty.—1st ed.
    p. cm.—(Primary sources in American history)
Includes bibliographical references and index.
ISBN 1-4042-0176-9 (library binding)
1. United States—Territorial expansion—Juvenile literature. 2. United States—
Ethnic relations—Juvenile literature.
I. Title. II. Series: Primary sources in American history (New York, N.Y.)
E179.5.M68 2004
979'.02—dc22

                                                                    2004003822

Manufactured in the United States of America

On the front cover: *American Progress*, an allegorical painting by John Gast
that portrays America's westward expansion as the advancement of civilization
across North America.

On the back cover: First row (left to right): John Bakken's sod house in Milton,
North Dakota; Oswego starch factory in Oswego, New York. Second row (left to
right): *American Progress*, painted by John Gast in 1872; the Battle of Palo Alto.
Third row (left to right): Pony Express rider pursued by Native Americans on the
plains; Union soldiers investigating the rubble of a Southern building.

CONTENTS

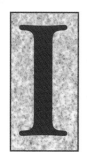NTRODUCTION

The United States' founders saw wilderness spread to the western horizon. It went as far as the eye could see, and much farther. At the time of the Constitution's signing in 1787, the young United States reached only as far west as the Appalachian Mountains. It covered an area of about 890,000 square miles (2.3 million square kilometers). Since then, the United States has added roughly 2.9 million square miles (7.5 million sq km). Today, the United States stretches from the Atlantic Ocean to the Pacific Ocean and includes the states of Hawaii and Alaska and other territories.

TO OVERSPREAD THE CONTINENT

Most of this territorial expansion occurred during the nineteenth century under the doctrine of Manifest Destiny. The term "Manifest Destiny" was popularized in 1845 by newspaper editor John O'Sullivan. It refers to the idea that it was America's God-given right and duty to expand its borders across the North American continent and, in the process, bring Christianity and democracy to more people. Urging the U.S. government to go to war with Mexico to settle a border dispute, O'Sullivan wrote that it was "our manifest destiny to overspread the continent allotted by Providence for the free development of our yearly multiplying millions."

Many Americans bought into or were inspired by the idea of a divine right to conquer North America. However, Manifest Destiny was primarily a justification for satisfying the United States' lust for land. Land represented wealth and progress to average Americans. The untapped wilderness before them provided an opportunity for economic advancement. On the national level, there were practical concerns for the desire for more land. These ranged from the need to protect national borders and the removal of foreign influences from the continent to providing more room for a growing population and facilitating trade with Asia.

Manifest Destiny was also a display of American nationalism and religious cultural arrogance, as well as a resolve to expand by any means necessary. The acquisition of additional territory was achieved in four ways: purchase, diplomacy, appropriation (or seizure), and war. At the end of the process, the United States had undergone tremendous growth and prosperity, paving the way for the nation's current status as a global superpower. However, Manifest Destiny brought mass destruction to the American Indian population and helped push the nation toward the Civil War.

TIMELINE

1787 — The Northwest Ordinance is passed, establishing a procedure by which territories could become states.

1803 — The Louisiana Purchase is completed, nearly doubling the size of the United States.

1819 — The United States acquires Florida with the signing of the Transcontinental Treaty.

1823 — James Monroe presents the Monroe Doctrine. The U.S. Supreme Court rules in *Johnson v. McIntosh* that American Indians have no land rights.

1836 — Texas draws up its Declaration of Independence from Mexico.

1842 — John Fremont explores California.

1845 — Texas becomes a state in the United States. John O'Sullivan coins the phrase "Manifest Destiny."

1846 — President Polk orders troops below the Nueces River, and the Mexican-American War begins.

TIMELINE

In California, John Fremont leads the Bear Flag Revolt. The United States comes to terms with Great Britain over the Oregon Territory.

1848 — The Mexican-American War ends. Mexico cedes the California Territory to the United States. James Marshall discovers gold in California.

1850 — California becomes a state.

1853 — The Gadsden Purchase is completed.

1861–1865 — The American Civil War is waged.

1867 — The United States purchases Alaska from Russia.

1875 — Hawaii and the United States sign a treaty of reciprocity.

1898 — The Spanish-American War ends. Spain cedes Puerto Rico, the Philippines, and Guam to the United States. The United States annexes Hawaii.

1914 — World War I begins, formally ending the Monroe Doctrine.

CHAPTER 1

Although the phrase "Manifest Destiny" was not used until 1845, the idea behind it can be traced all the way back to colonial America. In fact, one of the grievances that led to the Revolutionary War (1775–1783) was the colonists' resentment of Britain's prohibition on establishing settlements west of the Appalachian Mountains.

THE EARLY ACQUISITIONS

It was logical that, after winning its independence from Great Britain, the new nation would turn its attention to westward expansion. Accordingly, Congress passed the Land Ordinance in 1785 to promote the settlement of the Northwest Territory. The United States had acquired the territory from Great Britain at the end of the Revolutionary War. In 1787, Congress passed the Northwest Ordinance. This law established the procedures by which the Northwest Territory—and future territories—could become states in the Union. Over time, the Northwest Territory became the states of Ohio, Indiana,

The Northwest Ordinance of 1787 established that the Northwest Territory would eventually be organized into no less than three and no more than five states. In addition to setting up procedures by which territories could become states, it included provisions to fund education, outlaw slavery, and foster good relations with Indians living in the territory. Refer to page 55 for a partial transcription.

An ORDINANCE for the GOVERNMENT of the TERRITORY of the UNITED STATES, North-Weſt of the RIVER OHIO.

BE IT ORDAINED by the United States in Congreſs aſſembled, That the ſaid territory, for the purpoſes of tempo-rary government, be one diſtrict; ſubject, however, to be divided into two diſtricts, as future circumſtances may, in the opinion of Congreſs, make it expedient.

Be it ordained by the authority aforeſaid, That the eſtates both of reſident and non-reſident proprietors in the ſaid ter-ritory, dying inteſtate, ſhall deſcend to, and be diſtributed among their children, and the deſcendants of a deceaſed child in equal parts; the deſcendants of a deceaſed child or grand-child, to take the ſhare of their deceaſed parent in equal parts among them: And where there ſhall be no children or deſcendants, then in equal parts to the next of kin, in equal degree; and among collaterals, the children of a deceaſed brother or ſiſter of the inteſtate, ſhall have in equal parts among them their deceaſed parents ſhare; and there ſhall in no caſe be a diſtinction between kindred of the whole and half blood; ſa-ving in all caſes to the widow of the inteſtate, her third part of the real eſtate for life, and one third part of the perſonal eſtate; and this law relative to deſcents and dower, ſhall remain in full force until altered by the legiſlature of the diſ-trict.————And until the governor and judges ſhall adopt laws as herein after mentioned, eſtates in the ſaid territory may be deviſed or bequeathed by wills in writing, ſigned and ſealed by him or her, in whom the eſtate may be, (being of full age) and atteſted by three witneſſes; —and real eſtates may be conveyed by leaſe and releaſe, or bargain and ſale, ſigned, ſealed, and delivered by the perſon being of full age, in whom the eſtate may be, and atteſted by two wit-neſſes, provided ſuch wills be duly proved, and ſuch conveyances be acknowledged, or the execution thereof duly pro-ved, and be recorded within one year after proper magiſtrates, courts, and regiſters ſhall be appointed for that purpoſe; and perſonal property may be transferred by delivery, ſaving, however, to the French and Canadian inhabitants, and other ſettlers of the Kaskaskies, Saint Vincent's, and the neighbouring villages, who have heretofore profeſſed themſelves citizens of Virginia, their laws and cuſtoms now in force among them, relative to the deſcent and conveyance of pro-perty.

Be it ordained by the authority aforeſaid, That there ſhall be appointed from time to time, by Congreſs, a governor, whoſe commiſſion ſhall continue in force for the term of three years, unleſs ſooner revoked by Congreſs; he ſhall reſide in the diſtrict, and have a freehold eſtate therein, in one thouſand acres of land, while in the exerciſe of his office.

There ſhall be appointed from time to time, by Congreſs, a ſecretary, whoſe commiſſion ſhall continue in force for four years, unleſs ſooner revoked, he ſhall reſide in the diſtrict, and have a freehold eſtate therein, in five hundred acres of land, while in the exerciſe of his office; it ſhall be his duty to keep and preſerve the acts and laws paſſed by the le-giſlature, and the public records of the diſtrict, and the proceedings of the governor in his executive department; and tranſmit authentic copies of ſuch acts and proceedings, every ſix months, to the ſecretary of Congreſs: There ſhall al-ſo be appointed a court to conſiſt of three judges, any two of whom to form a court, who ſhall have a common law ju-riſdiction, and reſide in the diſtrict, and have each therein a freehold eſtate in five hundred acres of land, while in the exerciſe of their offices; and their commiſſions ſhall continue in force during good behaviour.

The governor and judges, or a majority of them, ſhall adopt and publiſh in the diſtrict, ſuch laws of the original ſtates, criminal and civil, as may be neceſſary, and beſt ſuited to the circumſtances of the diſtrict, and report them to Congreſs, from time to time, which laws ſhall be in force in the diſtrict until the organization of the general aſſembly therein, unleſs diſapproved of by Congreſs; but afterwards the legiſlature ſhall have authority to alter them as they ſhall think fit.

The governor for the time being, ſhall be commander in chief of the militia, appoint and commiſſion all officers in the ſame, below the rank of general officers; all general officers ſhall be appointed and commiſſioned by Congreſs.

Previous to the organization of the general aſſembly, the governor ſhall appoint ſuch magiſtrates and other civil of-ficers, in each county or townſhip, as he ſhall find neceſſary for the preſervation of the peace and good order in the ſame: After the general aſſembly ſhall be organized, the powers and duties of magiſtrates and other civil officers ſhall be regu-lated and defined by the ſaid aſſembly; but all magiſtrates and other civil officers, not herein otherwiſe directed, ſhall, during the continuance of this temporary government, be appointed by the governor.

For the prevention of crimes and injuries, the laws to be adopted or made ſhall have force in all parts of the diſtrict, and for the execution of proceſs, criminal and civil, the governor ſhall make proper diviſions thereof———and he ſhall proceed from time to time, as circumſtances may require, to lay out the parts of the diſtrict in which the Indian titles ſhall have been extinguiſhed, into counties and townſhips, ſubject, however, to ſuch alterations as may thereafter be made by the legiſlature.

So ſoon as there ſhall be five thouſand free male inhabitants, of full age, in the diſtrict, upon giving proof thereof to the governor, they ſhall receive authority, with time and place, to elect repreſentatives from their counties or town-ſhips, to repreſent them in the general aſſembly; provided that for every five hundred free male inhabitants there ſhall be one repreſentative, and ſo on progreſſively with the number of free male inhabitants, ſhall the right of repreſentation increaſe, until the number of repreſentatives ſhall amount to twenty-five, after which the number and proportion of re-preſentatives ſhall be regulated by the legiſlature; provided that no perſon be eligible or qualified to act as a repre-ſentative, unleſs he ſhall have been a citizen of one of the United States three years and be a reſident in the diſtrict, or unleſs he ſhall have reſided in the diſtrict three years, and in either caſe ſhall likewiſe hold in his own right, in fee ſim-ple, two hundred acres of land within the ſame:———Provided alſo, that a freehold in fifty acres of land in the diſtrict, having been a citizen of one of the ſtates, and being reſident in the diſtrict; or the like freehold and two years reſi-dence in the diſtrict ſhall be neceſſary to qualify a man as an elector of a repreſentative.

The repreſentatives thus elected, ſhall ſerve for the term of two years, and in caſe of the death of a repreſentative, or removal from office, the governor ſhall iſſue a writ to the county or townſhip for which he was a member, to elect another in his ſtead, to ſerve for the reſidue of the term.

The general aſſembly, or legiſlature, ſhall conſiſt of the governor, legiſlative council, and a houſe of repreſentatives. The legiſlative council ſhall conſiſt of five members, to continue in office five years, unleſs ſooner removed by Congreſs, any three of whom to be a quorum, and the members of the council ſhall be nominated and appointed in the following manner, to wit: As ſoon as repreſentatives ſhall be elected, the governor ſhall appoint a time and place for them to meet together, and, when met, they ſhall nominate ten perſons, reſidents in the diſtrict, and each poſſeſſed of a freehold in five hundred acres of land, and return their names to Congreſs; five of whom Congreſs ſhall appoint and commiſſion to ſerve as aforeſaid; and whenever a vacancy ſhall happen in the council, by death or removal from office, the houſe of repreſentatives ſhall nominate two perſons, qualified as aforeſaid, for each vacancy, and return their names to Con-greſs; one of whom Congreſs ſhall appoint and commiſſion for the reſidue of the term; and every five years, four months at leaſt before the expiration of the time of ſervice of the members of council, the ſaid houſe ſhall nominate ten perſons, qualified as aforeſaid, and return their names to Congreſs, five of whom Congreſs ſhall appoint and commiſſion to ſerve as members of the council five years, unleſs ſooner removed. And the governor, legiſlative council, and houſe of re-

Illinois, Michigan, and Wisconsin. The settlement and subsequent transformation of the Northwest Territory into states extended the U.S. border west to the Mississippi River.

The Louisiana Purchase

Thomas Jefferson became the third United States president in 1801. A longtime believer in the need to expand the nation's borders, Jefferson quickly set his sights on the French-held territory of Louisiana. He was particularly interested in its port city of New Orleans because it was at the mouth of the Mississippi River, which was a major commercial traffic route. Jefferson reasoned that if the United States could control New Orleans and the Mississippi River, it would lessen the chance of foreign interference in American trade.

In 1802, President Jefferson sent Robert Livingston to France with an offer to buy New Orleans for $2 million. At first, France declined the offer. However, in 1803, French dictator Napoléon Bonaparte, who needed money to finance his wars with other European countries, offered to sell the entire Louisiana Territory for $15 million. Livingston jumped at the offer. This transaction is known as the Louisiana Purchase.

The Louisiana Territory, which covered an area of 828,000 square miles (2.1 million sq km), stretched from the Mississippi River on the east to the Rocky Mountains on the west and from Canada in the north to the Gulf of Mexico in the south. Its acquisition nearly doubled the size of the country and reduced French power on the continent.

Having completed the Louisiana Purchase, President Jefferson sent an expedition, led by Meriwether Lewis and William Clark,

Thomas Jefferson is one of the most revered presidents in U.S. history. One of the Founding Fathers, he authored the Declaration of Independence at age thirty-three. Before becoming president in 1801, Jefferson was secretary of state in George Washington's administration and John Adams's vice president. Jefferson served two terms as president. The Louisiana Purchase was the most notable achievement of his presidency. This oil painting of Jefferson was created by Gilbert Stuart in 1805.

to explore the newly acquired lands. They were also instructed to make contact, form alliances, and establish trade with American Indians. In addition, they were to search for a mythical waterway called the Northwest Passage, which was believed to connect the Atlantic and Pacific Oceans. The reports from the expedition told of rich and fertile lands filled with natural resources. These reports whetted America's appetite for more land and adventure. Soon, American settlers flooded the Louisiana Territory, which over time became the states of Louisiana, Arkansas, Oklahoma, Missouri, Kansas, Nebraska, Iowa, South Dakota, Wyoming, Minnesota, Colorado, North Dakota, and Montana.

This 1803 map of North America shows the United States before the Louisiana Purchase. The Constitution did not expressly give the federal government the authority to acquire new territory. However, Jefferson believed that the advantages of purchasing the Louisiana Territory were so great that he was willing to risk violating the Constitution. Fortunately, the Senate agreed with him and willingly ratified the Louisiana Purchase Treaty.

The Acquisition of Florida

At the time of the Louisiana Purchase, there were two Floridas: East Florida and West Florida. East Florida included much of present-day Florida. West Florida occupied the strip of land on the Gulf Coast formed by parts of present-day Florida, Alabama, Mississippi, and Louisiana. Livingston had hoped to include West Florida in the Louisiana Purchase, but he found out that, like East Florida, it belonged to Spain. Upon learning this, Jefferson tried unsuccessfully to buy the Floridas from Spain.

This did not curb American interest in West Florida, however. American settlers moved into the area. Soon, a border dispute developed between the United States and Spain. Jefferson's successor, James Madison, claimed that West Florida had been part of the Louisiana Purchase—a claim that Spain refuted. In 1810, after a revolt by American settlers, who had always resisted Spanish control, Madison ordered the military occupation of the disputed area. Two years later, Congress formally annexed the region, even though Spain maintained its claim.

Meanwhile, Seminole Indians from East Florida were crossing into and conducting violent raids in the states of Georgia and South Carolina. This continued for several years. Spain was obliged to prevent these raids under a treaty it had signed with the United States in 1795, but it could not or would not do so. Finally, in 1817, President James Monroe authorized Andrew Jackson, commander of the American army in the Southwest, to lead a raid into East Florida to put an end to the Seminole threat. In 1818, Jackson not only destroyed Seminole settlements, but, without authorization, he also captured the capital

of Pensacola and the Spanish fort of St. Marks. This show of force eventually convinced Spain to yield its claim to West Florida and to cede (give) East Florida to the United States in exchange for $5 million in the Transcontinental Treaty of 1819.

In the negotiations leading to the Transcontinental Treaty, the United States had threatened all-out war with Spain and the seizure of not only East Florida but also Texas, which was also under Spanish control. Texas had long been a goal of American expansionists, many of whom incorrectly asserted it to have been a part of the Louisiana Purchase. In signing the Transcontinental Treaty, the United States yielded its claim to Texas. It also agreed to clearly defined borders between the

United States and New Spain (the name of the Spanish-held territory in North America).

Spain's hold on its North American territories, however, soon proved to be shaky. The situation would eventually lead to further American expansion.

The Monroe Doctrine

The growth of the United States made it a more important player in global politics. As a result, the United States felt the need to define its foreign policies. In December 1823, James Monroe announced what would become a primary force in Manifest Destiny: the Monroe Doctrine. This shaped the United States' foreign policy through the beginning of the twentieth century. The Monroe Doctrine stated that the United States would stay out of European affairs, but only if European countries would stay out of American affairs. By American affairs, the United States meant developments in all of the Americas: North America, South America, and the Caribbean. With the Monroe Doctrine, the United States announced its intention to be the dominant influence in the region.

CHAPTER 2

By the early nineteenth century, Texas already had a rich history. For centuries, the grassy expanse was home to a number of Native American tribes. The Caddo, who lived near present-day Dallas, were peaceful farmers. The Karankawa were a fishing people who lived off the Gulf Coast in southeast Texas. The Apache and the Comanche occupied the west, where they hunted buffalo and battled each other. Smaller tribes also lived along the banks of the Rio Grande in the south, while nomads roamed the state.

THE ANNEXATION OF TEXAS

Between the late 1600s and 1821, Texas was under Spanish control as part of New Spain. It served as an outpost for Spanish explorers and traders on their way west. In 1821, New Spain won its independence from Spain and became Mexico.

American Settlers in Mexico

By that time, Americans had already begun establishing settlements in Texas. In 1820, Moses Austin, who had received a land grant from Spain, began a colony of Anglo-American (Americans of English descent) settlers in Texas. When he died the following year, his son Stephen took over the management of the colony.

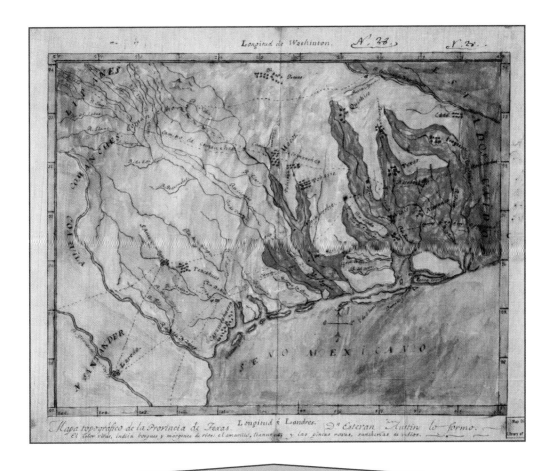

This map of Texas was drawn by Stephen Austin in 1822. It is drawn on cloth and labeled in Spanish. Austin became known as the father of Texas. He persuaded many American settlers to move to Texas during the early nineteenth century and worked closely with the Mexican government to facilitate the settlements.

The government of Mexico was concerned that its northern territories—primarily Texas—were underpopulated. For various reasons, including constant warfare with American Indians and the inability of the military to guard the borderlands, it could not convince Mexicans to relocate there. Consequently, the Mexican government encouraged more Americans to settle the region by offering them large tracts of fertile land at a relatively cheap price. However, the settlers were required to follow a number of rules. These included learning to speak Spanish, converting to Catholicism, becoming Mexican citizens, obeying Mexican law, and observing a ban on slavery.

Word spread of the rich land, and thousands of settlers poured across the border. Throughout the South, people abandoned their homes, carving the letters GTT in their doors: Gone to Texas. By 1830, there were more than 20,000 Americans living in Texas, greatly outnumbering the native Texans, called Tejanos.

Texas Becomes Independent

Friction soon developed between the settlers and the Tejanos, who resented the land grants to the Americans. Moreover, the settlers ran into disagreement with the Mexican government, primarily because they generally ignored the rules they had agreed to in accepting the settlements. Few learned to speak Spanish. Fewer still truly converted to Catholicism. Most continued to identify themselves as Americans rather than as Mexican citizens, and many illegally owned slaves. In addition, many smuggled in American-made goods to avoid paying duties on imported products. They resented the Mexican government, which in 1830 was run by a dictator. Worried about the increasing immigrant population in Texas, the Mexican government passed the Law of April 6 in 1830, which halted immigration. This law angered the settlers, many of whom called for a revolution.

In the winter of 1833, Stephen Austin traveled to Mexico City to present the settlers' grievances to President Antonio López de Santa Anna. Santa Anna agreed to Austin's demands, which

Stephen Austin was born in Wythe County, Virginia, on November 3, 1793. He held several important jobs before moving to Texas. These included Missouri territorial legislator, director of the Bank of St. Louis, and circuit judge of the first judicial district of Arkansas. He was also editor of a New Orleans newspaper. In Texas, he was the empresario, or administrative authority. As such, he was responsible for controlling immigration, setting up a law-enforcement system, and developing public facilities such as roads, schools, and mills. After the Texas revolution, he ran unsuccessfully for president of Texas.

included limited self-government. However, as Austin was returning to Texas, Santa Anna had him jailed for treason. Texas immigrants like Samuel Houston and Davy Crockett immediately called for complete independence from Mexico.

The Texas revolution began in October 1835. By the following spring, the insurgent leaders had drafted the Texas Declaration of Independence as well as a constitution. American volunteers teemed over the border with the promise of land at four cents an acre (10 cents per hectare). Santa Anna sent troops marching into San Antonio, Texas. The Mexican forces cornered a group of the radical Americans in the Alamo. After a two-week

The Texas Declaration of Independence was passed unanimously by the delegates at the General Convention of 1836 on March 2. Drafted in less than a day, it mirrors the American Declaration of Independence in many ways. While it was being prepared, the Mexican army was attacking the Alamo in San Antonio. Refer to pages 55–56 for a partial transcription.

standoff, the Mexican army broke through. It slaughtered the 188 Anglo-Texan soldiers, including Crockett.

A month later, a band of Anglo-Texans surprised the sleeping Mexican army near the San Jacinto River. They overpowered the soldiers easily. Santa Anna was forced to sign the Texas Declaration of Independence. Texas became its own country. Santa Anna also signed a treaty recognizing the Rio Grande as the new nation's southernmost border. Although the Mexican congress rejected the agreement, it recognized Texas's independence. However, it claimed that the southern border was actually the Nueces River, 150 miles (241 km) to the north. This would become an important issue several years later.

Annexation

Once Texas declared independence from Mexico, the United States immediately recognized it as a country. To many Americans, it seemed logical that Texas would someday become a state. Likewise, the Texans expressed their interest in joining the United States. However, the Texans had more immediate concerns. There were Mexican border raids. Their money was practically worthless. The government was deeply in debt.

The question of admitting Texas into the United States was a tricky one, primarily because of the divisive issue of slavery. The annexation of Texas became a major political issue. If Texas were admitted to the Union, it would disrupt the delicate balance of slave states and free states. Southern states, where slavery was legal and almost universally practiced, pushed for annexation. Northern states and abolitionists, people who advocated an end to slavery, opposed it. The issue

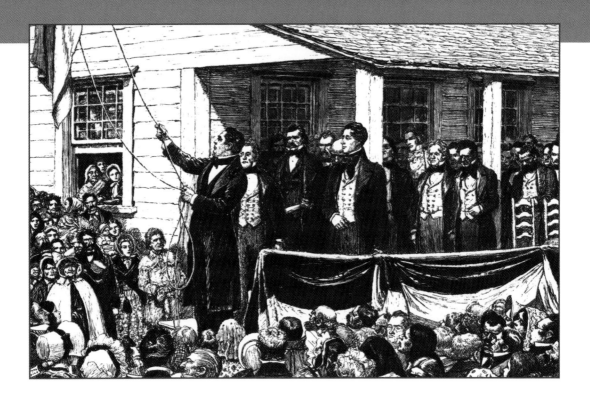

This print shows Texas president Anson Jones lowering the Texan flag following annexation by the United States in 1845. Born in Massachusetts in 1798, Jones moved to Texas in 1833. He served in Texas's revolutionary army during the revolution. Jones served as a congressman and later as an ambassador before becoming president of an independent Texas. He was unenthusiastic about annexation and lost influence in the republic as a result. He failed in several attempts to be elected to public office after Texas became a state.

would not be resolved for another nine years, during which the leaders of the fledgling nation debated the merits of joining the United States.

Texas became an issue during the presidential campaign of 1844. Presidential candidate James K. Polk argued in favor of annexation. He promised to annex Texas immediately if elected. If the United States did not annex Texas, he argued, England would. His position gained him the valuable votes of the South. Polk won the election by a narrow margin.

Early in 1845, before Polk took office, Congress passed a bill approving the annexation of Texas. John Tyler, who was president at the time, signed the bill into law on March 1. Mexico had threatened to go to war with the United States if Texas was annexed. It immediately cut off formal relations with the United States.

The first year of Polk's presidency was filled with political wrangling. Although annexation had been approved, whether Texas would enter the Union as a slave state was still up in the air. Also in question was the southern boundary of Texas. Was it at the Rio Grande as the Texans claimed or the Nueces River as Mexico insisted? The U.S. Senate resolved to do nothing. It left the boundary open to future negotiation with Mexico.

Finally, the slavery issue was resolved with a simple solution. Texas would be admitted into the Union as a slave state. However, in order to balance it out, Oregon would be admitted as a free state. On December 29, 1845, Texas officially became the twenty-eighth state.

CHAPTER 3

At the end of the eighteenth century, the Oregon Territory was fully occupied. Various American Indian tribes had been living in the region for thousands of years. They included the Clatsop, Chetco, Takelma, and Shasta. The environment was predominantly wooded. Rivers cut through to the sea. The rivers brimmed with salmon and other fish. The American Indians used cedar trees to build their houses and canoes. The woods provided berries and animals for food and clothing. In the high desert inland, American Indians roamed the Oregon Territory in an annual 200-mile (322 km) cycle.

MANIFEST DESTINY IN THE PACIFIC NORTHWEST

Competing Claims

As explorers visited the area from the fifteenth century on, various countries laid claim to the Oregon Territory, ignoring the American Indians who had been there first. It was originally claimed by Spain as part of an overall claim on North America. Russia later asserted that it was part of Alaska, which it owned until 1867. Britain claimed it after it was visited by several British explorers, including Sir Alexander MacKenzie and George

Vancouver, in the 1790s. The United States based its right to the territory on the Lewis and Clark expedition that explored it in 1805. In 1818, the United States and Great Britain agreed to jointly occupy and administer the Oregon Territory. By the mid-1820s, only the British and American claims remained.

Settlers Arrive

During the first years of the nineteenth century, following the Lewis and Clark expedition, settlers slowly began to trickle into the Oregon Territory. Most of them came from the eastern United States. Others came from Canada, which was then British territory. The area was especially popular with fur trappers. Religious missionaries also moved in to convert American Indians to Christianity, which they saw as a more civilized religion. Lured by descriptions of a rich land, businessmen began to make grand plans. Large companies began to send teams west.

Soon, companies like the British Hudson's Bay Company moved in. Hudson's Bay Company set up elaborate trading posts. In the process, it defined a new balance of life in the Pacific Northwest. At the posts, American Indians traded furs in return for manufactured goods imported from the East. Settlers created a network of forts, laced together by the region's numerous rivers. They laid out orchards, planted gardens, and began to cultivate the land. Men cut lumber and began to build settlements. They coexisted relatively comfortably with the American Indians who had lived there long before.

Just as reports of Lewis and Clark's trip had spread back east, so did news of the success of Hudson's Bay Company. Life on the frontier attracted a peculiar array of men and women. Some wanted a fresh start in life after struggling financially in the East.

This engraving depicts the fur trading post at Astoria in the Oregon Territory around 1813. Astoria was founded in 1811 by German merchant John Jacob Astor, who organized the Pacific Fur Company. It was also the first permanent U.S. settlement on the Pacific Coast. During the War of 1812, the British blockaded the post. Frustrated, Astor sold it to the British in 1813. Fort Astoria came back under American control in the mid-1840s.

Others were enterprising businesspeople. Some were visionaries, wanting to create a new kind of life on the fringe of society.

Hall Jackson Kelley was a schoolteacher from Massachusetts. He thought that life in the Northwest could be a utopia—an ideal society. He preached of the "spontaneous growth of the soil" and the "fruits of laborious industry." Eventually, his utopia was tied to the financial scheme of Nathaniel Jarvis Wyeth, a Boston merchant. The plan eventually evolved into the Pacific

Trading Company. Wyeth wanted to set up a trading post to ship furs to Asia. Though the Pacific Trading Company failed, it was indicative of the optimism surrounding the region. In 1827, the United States and Britain renewed their agreement to coexist in the Oregon Territory.

Negotiating for the Oregon Territory

Throughout the 1840s, Oregon conventions met all across the West. The purpose of the conventions was to discuss taking over the Oregon Territory. Participants demanded that the United States once and for all claim Oregon for itself. They argued that a country like Britain could never use or govern the land effectively. President James Polk answered their call.

When Polk entered office in 1845, he declared that the United States' right to Oregon was "clear and unquestionable." Polk announced, "Already are our people preparing to perfect [the claim] by occupying it with their wives and children." The reality was not so simple. First, there was the issue of Britain's competing claim. Also, the Oregon Territory was huge. It was made up of what are now Oregon, Washington, Idaho, and parts of Montana, Wyoming, and British Columbia, Canada. For those on the East Coast, it lay in the unimaginable distance. It was on the other side of thousands of miles of raw wilderness.

But the government provided incentive for people to move there in the form of 1,000 free acres (405 ha). Travelers excitedly forged a path to the Northwest. The Oregon Trail was a long and treacherous road. Many potential settlers perished along the way. The 2,000-mile (3,219 km) unpaved highway from the Midwest cut straight through American Indian territories. More than 3,000 people arrived in Oregon in 1845. By this point, many American

President James Knox Polk served only one term in office, between 1845 and 1849. He was the eleventh president of the United States. As he had promised, he did not seek reelection, although he was immensely popular. Still, he remains one of the most successful presidents in U.S. history. He accomplished all the major items on his political agenda, including the annexation of Texas and the settlement of the dispute with Britain over the Oregon question. He died three months after leaving office. This portrait of Polk was created by Currier & Ives during his presidency.

Indians had become increasingly upset about the settlements. They frequently attacked those who passed through.

Polk opened negotiations with Britain over the Oregon Territory in the summer of 1845. He initially proposed dividing the territory between the two countries, setting the boundary at the forty-ninth parallel. When Britain rejected his proposal, Polk withdrew from the negotiations and called on Congress to void the joint occupancy agreement within a year. Polk's response was provocative and risked an outbreak of war between the two powers—a war that neither side wanted. Eventually, Britain relented and agreed to set the boundary at the forty-ninth parallel, the current boundary with Canada. The U.S. Senate approved the treaty in 1846.

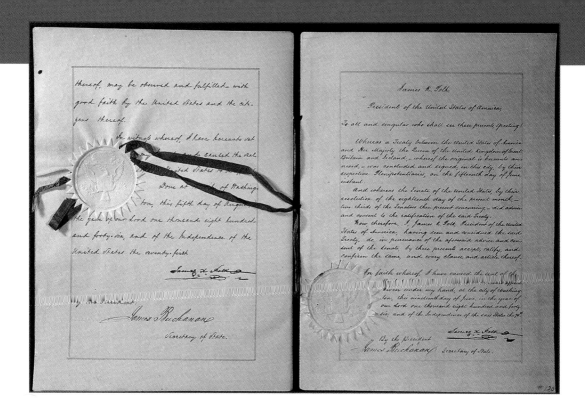

This is the Oregon Treaty of 1846, which divided the Oregon Territory between the United States and Britain. Although the agreement set the border at the forty-ninth parallel, Vancouver Island, which is south of the forty-ninth parallel, was given to the British. An ambiguity in the wording of the treaty led to the Pig War of 1859 over the ownership of the San Juan Islands. The Pig War was so called because the only casualty of the military standoff was a pig. Refer to page 56 for a partial transcription.

Settlers poured into the Oregon Territory following the deal. By 1850, the population had topped 9,000. It was the first great migration in American history. The settlers established governments like those in the East. They built houses to look like those they had left, frequently ignoring the requirements of the climate. Still, they succeeded.

Though the Oregon Territory was absorbed, the going would not be easy for settlers. The land may have technically belonged

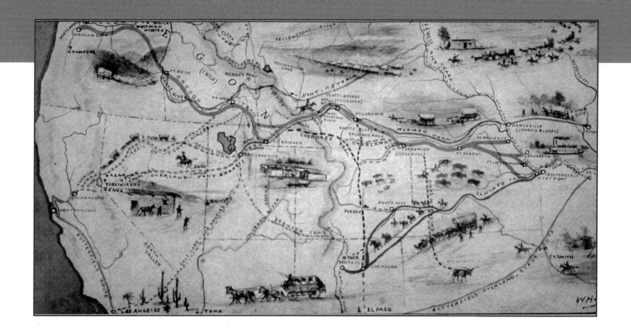

This circa 1840 map shows the westward trail from Missouri to Oregon. The Oregon Trail was considerably trying for settlers. Roughly one in ten died along the way. Many settlers walked the 2,000-mile pathway, which ran across mountains, barefoot. They traveled in dread of Indian attacks, which were actually very rare. Most of the casualties among the settlers were a result of cholera, drowning, accidents, and illness caused by poor sanitation.

to the United States, but one would be hard-pressed to tell the American Indians. In the decades after Oregon's annexation, there were several Indian uprisings. Each was brutally put down. The United States moved into the land wholeheartedly, establishing federal projects.

With the question of the Oregon Territory settled, the energy of Manifest Destiny rolled onward. President Polk had set his sights on Mexico. Specifically, he lusted after the gleaming coastline below Oregon: California. The road there was long. And it began back in Texas.

CHAPTER 4

President James K. Polk had long lusted after California. According to Jeanne Boydston in *Making a Nation: The United States and Its People*, Polk confided to Missouri senator Thomas Hart Benton in 1845 that he "had California and the fine bay of San Francisco as much in view as Oregon" when he made expansionism the main focus of his presidential campaign. There was, however, a crucial obstacle: California belonged to Mexico.

DREAMS OF CALIFORNIA LEAD TO WAR

The Allure of California

Myth formed the basis for much of Manifest Destiny, and the history of California was filled with myths. The earliest European explorers thought they might find the fabled Northwest Passage on California's Pacific coast. Barring that, they believed they would at least find riches beyond their wildest dreams.

The name "California" was drawn from a novel by sixteenth-century writer Garcia Rodriguez de Montalvo. "There is an island called California, very close to that part of the Terrestrial Paradise," he wrote. The American Indians' arms were "all of gold, as [are] the harnesses of the wild beasts which, after taming, they ride. In all the island, there is no other metal."

The Santa Barbara mission in California was founded by father Fermin Lasuen on December 4, 1786. The friendly Chumash Indians of the region helped in its construction. Called the Queen of the Missions, the Santa Barbara mission survived on agriculture. Its priests and the Indians they employed raised thousands of head of cattle and grew crops of wheat, corn, barley, and beans. This watercolor painting of the Santa Barbara mission was created by Henry Chapman Ford around the early 1880s.

Spanish Missions

In the mid-sixteenth century, Spanish explorer Juan Rodriguez Cabrillo sailed to California from what was still New Spain. His ships went up the coast to present-day Los Angeles. By the mid-eighteenth century, there were Spanish settlements up and down the coast. Many of these settlements were based around missions.

Junípero Serra founded the California mission system in 1769. He led what was dubbed the Sacred Expedition. Nine missions were constructed along the California coast, each a day's ride

Father Junípero Serra was born Miguel José Serra in Majorca, Spain, in 1713. He joined the Franciscan Order of the Catholic Church when he was sixteen years old. He was ordained as a priest shortly thereafter, at which point he assumed the name Junípero. Serra arrived in New Spain in 1750, where he worked at a mission near Mexico City for seventeen years. He moved to present-day California in 1767, where he founded nine missions. Serra suffered many personal sacrifices while developing the missions. He often clashed with religious and political authorities over funding and other concerns. His missions were economically successful, producing enough surplus cattle and grain to trade with Mexico.

from the next. The primary goal of the mission system was to convert American Indians to Roman Catholicism. However, the Spaniards also believed that they should socialize the Indians. They schooled the Indians in the Spanish way of life, from language to dress to work habits.

The missions were not entirely popular with American Indians. In order to defend the missions against Indian attacks, the Spanish constructed forts called presidios. The government founded towns called pueblos in order to ensure a food supply for the presidios. The government enticed potential residents with free land, animals, equipment, and money.

Following the Mexican Revolution in the early nineteenth century, the missions were made secular, or nonreligious. Instead of being religious centers, they simply became points of trade. Many Mexican businessmen established huge cattle ranches. The American Indians became a cheap source of labor.

American Settlers

In 1826, the first American settlers crossed the Mojave Desert and the San Bernardino Mountains. They arrived at the mission in San Gabriel. Soon, they moved north into the Central Valley. They discovered that it was a trapper's heaven. After they returned east, a steady flow of eager businessmen began to head for California. As in Oregon, travelers soon published their findings. "There can be no better [climate] in the world," Richard Henry Dana wrote in his book *Two Years Before the Mast.* "In the hands of an enterprising people, what a country this might be!"

In 1842, John Fremont of the Army Corps of Technical Engineers began to explore California. He had traveled south from the Oregon Territory. With his wife, he wrote several best-selling accounts of his trip. Because he traveled predominantly in the northern part of the territory, he saw very little Mexican control. His accounts enticed other American settlers to move into the area and excited expansionist politicians.

The Mexican-American War

In 1845, the United States offered Mexico $40 million in return for California. Special commissioner John Slidell traveled to Mexico City to negotiate. Using the ongoing Texas border dispute as an excuse, Polk also sent troops to Texas. So while Slidell negotiated, the troops hovered menacingly at the border.

John Charles Fremont was born in Savannah, Georgia, on January 21, 1813. He was one of the most successful explorers of the nineteenth century. An advocate for westward expansion, he participated in, and even led, various expeditions, mapping unsettled territories or surveying prospective railroad routes. His many explorations earned him the nickname "the pathfinder." Fremont ran unsuccessfully for president in 1856. He was appointed as a major general of the Union army at the outbreak of the Civil War. He soon lost his post for declaring that all slaves owned by Confederates in Missouri were free. He served as governor of the Arizona Territory between 1878 and 1881.

Nevertheless, Mexico rejected the United States' offer. Polk believed that a "small war" would change Mexico's position.

More than 4,000 soldiers—half the U.S. Army—under the command of General Zachary Taylor made winter camp at Corpus Christi, south of the Nueces disputed territory. Even Texans agreed that if the army crossed the boundary, it might be considered an act of war. Nevertheless, in early 1846, Polk ordered the soldiers on. Taylor and his men advanced into the disputed zone.

The troops had dragged cannons and weapons across desolate miles. They aimed them at the town of Matamoros, across the river. American soldiers were unruly. They desecrated local churches and attacked worshipers. Taylor struggled to keep discipline. Mexican authorities sent letters of protest to the United States government.

In early April, the situation reached a boiling point. The commander of the Mexican army sent a note to Taylor ordering him to retreat. Taylor responded by ordering a naval blockade at the mouth of the Rio Grande. The Mexicans considered it a hostile act. They sent 1,600 troops across the river. On April 26, they killed eleven American dragoons (soldiers on horseback). General Taylor sent a letter to President Polk stating that the war was on.

Taylor's letter set off a brief and fiery debate in Congress. Legislators eventually passed the war bill. But news traveled slowly in those days, and Taylor had continued to fight without waiting for word from Washington. The United States Army and Navy were poorly prepared for the war, however. Except for brief battles with American Indians, they had not fought since 1815, when the War of 1812 ended. The troops fought raggedly. Instead of training them further, Taylor was forced to spend time tracking down supplies. American troops continued to run amok. They robbed Mexican farmers of their cattle and corn.

As the battles raged, President Polk was covertly plotting an end to the war with Santa Anna. After his defeat in Texas, Santa Anna was exiled to Cuba. However, he wanted to return to power. He entered into a deal with the United States government. If the United States would help him regain the Mexican presidency, he would help it win the war in Texas. He promised not only to recognize the Rio Grande as the border but to cede most of California to the United States. Polk

Antonio López de Santa Anna was born in Veracruz, Mexico, on February 21, 1794. He joined the army at age sixteen and soon distinguished himself as a military officer. He was elected president of Mexico in 1833 but almost immediately installed himself as dictator. Between 1833 and 1855, he served eleven nonconsecutive terms as president of an unstable country that underwent thirty-six changes in the presidency. During that period, Santa Anna was twice forced into exile.

agreed. The United States would support the general's return and would even pay him.

Santa Anna suggested that the United States first depose General Mariano Paredes, the Mexican president. This would leave a vacuum in the Mexican government, and the Mexicans would welcome Santa Anna back with open arms. It would be in the United States' interest to have a United States–controlled leader in Mexico City. Polk needed to raise money. He asked Congress for $2 million to support the war effort and to pay off Santa Anna. The bill was rejected in Congress.

The Nation Debates the War

The debate over the war raged in the United States. The two sides of the debate were called "cotton" and "conscience." The former were those in favor of the war. As expansionists, their support of the war was tied to their wish to expand the country. Their wish to expand was, in turn, connected to their hope that slavery would spread westward. Those on the side of conscience believed that the war was wrong. They believed that expansionism was wrong, and they certainly believed that slavery was wrong.

In Mexico, the war dragged on. Taylor pushed his troops. Despite numerous setbacks, President Paredes fell. The new Mexican government wished to continue the war. It invited Santa Anna back. By the end of the summer, Santa Anna had returned to Mexico City. Though he did not immediately regain the presidency, he was granted a high military post. Almost as soon as he returned, he double-crossed the United States. Suddenly, he bragged that he had 25,000 men ready to do battle with and defeat the United States' forces. He had nothing of the sort. It would take him until January 1847 to muster even 18,000 troops. Nonetheless, he had returned to power. Instead of extinguishing the war, he had fueled the flames.

Success Despite Poor Preparations

General Taylor was oblivious to Washington's plans. He continued to battle valiantly on the front. He suffered many setbacks before finally taking the provincial town of Monterrey. Mexico City was far away. Taylor needed to regroup. Polk sent him new orders. The president and others disagreed with how Taylor was handling the fighting. Furious messages were sent back and forth. Miscommunication was rampant. Sometimes, Taylor ignored Polk's orders. Sometimes, he simply never received them. Once, Mexican forces intercepted letters from Washington. The letters ordered the army to invade the port of Tampico. The Mexicans rushed to defend it. Since the U.S. forces never received the orders, though, they never invaded.

Taylor was having some success. Northern Mexico was secure. Polk, however, needed the war to move faster. Many were campaigning against the war on the home front and were turning against the idea of aggressive expansionism. General Winfield Scott, Taylor's rival, proposed a strategy. New recruits, 10,000 of them, in addition to 20,000 troops already in Mexico, would be dispatched along the Brazos River. From there, they would capture Veracruz. Then, they would move west, inland, to Mexico City. In November, Polk approved Scott's plan.

Political intrigue filled Congress and the War Department. Furious at Taylor, Polk made Scott the head of the war operation.

Top: A portrait of Major General Winfield Scott in Veracruz, Mexico, on March 25, 1847. Bottom: A lithograph portraying the Battle of Buena Vista, in which the American army under the command of General Zachary Taylor was victorious. Taylor lost his command to Scott in early 1847.

However, he included many of Taylor's troops among the numbers to be transferred to Scott. In February 1847, Santa Anna's men surrounded Taylor and his 4,800 remaining troops at Buena Vista. Santa Anna had a force of more than 18,000. The Mexicans bore down on the Americans. Despite being massively outnumbered, U.S. soldiers drove back the Mexicans with artillery fire. After the second day of fighting, they expected to be defeated. When they woke, though, they discovered that Santa Anna and his men had fled in the night. The news was excitedly received in the United States.

Meanwhile, small rebellions shook Mexico. Santa Anna became president. His first task was to deal with the rebellions. Veracruz was left virtually undefended. Scott and his men took it easily, and the city was all but destroyed. Most of the casualties were civilians, including many women and children. When the news spread, many were shocked by the destruction. It fueled more antiwar movements throughout the United States. Despite this, Scott pressed on.

Though he had no authority to do so, Santa Anna began to negotiate with the Americans. He actually asked Scott to advance toward Mexico City so that he might pressure the Mexican congress into allowing him to make a peace treaty. He convinced Americans to give him $10,000 in cash. The battle for Mexico City was bloody. More than 4,000 Mexicans and 1,000 Americans were slaughtered. In September 1847, the United States took the city.

The California Front

While the Mexican-American War was fought mostly south of the Rio Grande, some battles raged in California. John Fremont instigated what became known as the Bear Flag Revolt. Though he had no official orders from the United States government, he attempted to seize California in the name of the country. He succeeded in capturing Colonel Mariano Guadalupe Vallejo. Soon, however, the United States Navy descended on the coast. The Mexicans put up a good fight, but the United States easily won California.

The Treaty of Guadalupe Hidalgo

The peace process was long and complicated. Both the Mexican congress and the U.S. Congress bickered internally. President Polk ordered Nicholas Trist, his chief negotiator, to step down. Trist ignored him. In January 1848, Trist began formal negotiations. In early February, he signed the Treaty of Guadalupe Hidalgo. The treaty set the Texas boundary at the Rio Grande. Also, for $15 million, it granted the United States 525,000 square miles (1.4 million sq km) of territory that included present-day Arizona, western Colorado, Nevada, New Mexico, and Utah, as well as California.

California was the grand prize of Manifest Destiny. It was at the far end of the North American continent. To many, it represented the United States grown to its full potential. More significant, it also linked the United States with Asia. Newspaper editors across the country encouraged enterprising men to "Go West!" As it had been before the war, California was thought of as a land of boundless natural resources.

This notion was soon partially proved right. In January 1848, James Marshall discovered gold outside of San Francisco. News spread quickly to the city. From there, news rippled outward. Across the country, people caught gold fever. Tens of thousands of people headed west in search of the rare metal. They

This is the first page from the Treaty of Guadalupe Hidalgo. Signed on February 2, 1848, it ended the war between the United States and Mexico. By its terms, Mexico gave up 55 percent of its territory for $15 million. However, the United States agreed to honor the property rights of the inhabitants of the territory it acquired. The Senate approved the treaty on March 10, 1848. Refer to pages 56–57 for a partial transcription.

dropped everything. In 1848, San Francisco was a small town of 600 people. By 1849, its population had zoomed up to more than 25,000. San Francisco was a boomtown. All across the state, new towns practically burst out of the ground. Old towns became cities. Tent metropolises sprung up amid half-finished buildings. The atmosphere was dreamlike. Because everything had happened so quickly, San Francisco's political system was often disorganized.

California wished to apply for statehood. As with Texas, slavery was an issue. California insisted that it be admitted as a free state. This angered senators from the South. It would upset the balance of free and slave states. A compromise was reached in Congress. A strict fugitive slave law was passed, and California was admitted as a free state.

Although the doctrine of Manifest Destiny had expanded the United States' border to the Pacific, it was not yet over. The Monroe Doctrine would be in place until the United States' entrance into World War I. Before then, the country continued to move west, now into the Pacific Ocean.

 HAPTER 5

In 1853, the United States purchased a small piece of land (29,000 square miles, or 75,110 sq km) from Mexico for $10 million. The land was bought to facilitate building a transcontinental railroad to California and keeping the tracks totally within the United States' borders. The transaction is known as the Gadsden Purchase. It was named for railroad developer James Gadsden, who negotiated the deal.

COMPLETING THE PICTURE

President Franklin Pierce had desired a more substantial portion of northern Mexican territory and had authorized Gadsden to spend up to $50 million to secure it. Gadsden was successful in negotiating for more land. However, senators representing northern states led a successful movement in Congress to reject much of the land that Mexico was willing to sell.

With the Gadsden Purchase, the last piece of territory was added to the continental United States. Many historians view it as having marked the end of Manifest Destiny. However, the United States would later acquire additional territories.

Alaska

Alaska sits on the far northwestern corner of North America. It had been settled by Russia during the early eighteenth century. However, Russia lacked the financial resources to maintain major settlements or establish a military presence there. The Russian government offered to sell the Alaska territory to the United States in 1866. William H. Seward, the U.S. secretary of state, wanted the United States to acquire the territory so much that he began negotiations before he got permission from President Andrew Johnson. Seward was an advocate of continued U.S. expansion. The following year, Seward and Russian minister Edouard de Stoeckl agreed on the price. The United States bought Alaska's 586,400 square miles (1.5 million sq km) for $7.2 million.

Seward worked hard to overcome significant resistance to the transaction in Congress. Opponents ridiculed the purchase as "Seward's folly" and referred to Alaska as "Seward's icebox." However, Congress approved the deal, and on October 18, 1867, Alaska officially became a territory of the United States. The discovery of gold in Alaska in 1896 eventually silenced Seward's critics.

Hawaii

Hawaii had been on maps since the late eighteenth century. Captain James Cook of England had explored it and named it the Sandwich Islands.

When Europeans first arrived in Hawaii, Hawaiian culture was long established. The native people on the island, the Kanaka Maoli, lived peacefully and numbered well into the hundreds of thousands. The Kanaka Maoli had a very different value system than did the European settlers. They did not believe in

The United States purchased Alaska from Russia for $7.2 million with this check. It was made payable to Edouard de Stoeckl, who negotiated the deal for the Russians. The purchase agreement included a provision that Alaska's Russian settlers could return to Russia within three years. However, those that chose to remain would enjoy all the rights of American citizens.

land ownership. They shared everything. They called the land Papa, which means Earth mother. To the Kanaka Maoli, the idea of owning part of Papa was ludicrous.

Cook's arrival spurred nationalism among the Kanaka Maoli. King Kamehameha united the Hawaiian Islands as one kingdom. Later, the Kanaka Maoli killed Cook as he returned to shore.

During the early nineteenth century, Hawaii became an important trading port between Asia and the west coast of North America. Asian silks and spices were sent east, while American furs were sent west. In addition, the islands became the center of the Pacific whaling industry.

During the early 1840s, whaling began to decline. When this happened, sugarcane became the primary crop on the islands. As had happened in the early settlements in California, the settlers all but enslaved the native people to work the fields.

This illustration from around 1820 portrays Hawaiian king Kamehameha surrounded by some of his subjects. In it, King Kamehameha wears a western suit, unlike his subjects who are clothed in traditional dress. The king's attire may reflect the close relationship that he had with the American and British traders who had helped him defeat a rival— and the true heir to the throne—in the Hawaiian Wars of 1785–1792. He was known as Kamehameha the Great for his prowess as a warrior and his skills as a statesman. His unification of Hawaii brought peace and prosperity to the kingdom.

Sugar was big business in Hawaii. Many European nations wanted to annex Hawaii. Many of the businessmen in Hawaii had come from the United States. They believed that the United States should be the country to absorb Hawaii. In 1875, Hawaii and the United States signed a treaty of reciprocity. Technically, Hawaii was still a monarchy, but American influences continued to grow there. As a result, Americans began to invest even more in Hawaii.

This caused some amount of conflict between native Hawaiians and the settlers. In 1889, the islanders staged an uprising. They protested the constitution that King Kalakaua had been forced to sign in 1887. The rebellion was put down. In 1894, Hawaii was established as a republic. In 1898, the United States took Hawaii formally under its control. Finally, in 1900, Hawaii became a territory of the United States. It became a state in 1959.

Other Territories

The United States acquired a number of other territories around the turn of the twentieth century. These acquisitions were realized either by direct purchases or in the terms of treaties signed to end military conflicts.

The Spanish-American War

On January 25, 1898, the American ship USS *Maine* entered the harbor in Havana, Cuba, to protect American interests as Cuba struggled for independence from Spain. Almost three weeks later, the ship was blown up, killing 254 seamen and injuring 59. The U.S. Navy conducted an investigation into the explosion but could not determine who was responsible. However, many newspapers blamed Spain. To many Americans, this seemed a logical conclusion because the United States was supporting Cuban independence.

On April 25, the United States declared war on Spain. This war is known as the Spanish-American War. The war, which lasted several months, was fought in Cuba, Puerto Rico, and the Philippines. The Spanish-American War ended with the signing of the Treaty of Paris on December 10, 1898. In the treaty, the defeated Spain gave Puerto Rico and Guam to the United States. In addition, Spain sold the Philippines to the United States for $20 million.

Almost immediately, Filipinos resisted American rule. Between 1899 and 1903, the United States was engaged in a bloody conflict with Filipino forces, which it eventually overwhelmed. The Philippines finally became independent in 1946.

Puerto Rico and Guam continue to be U.S. territories. In all, the United States has fourteen territories. These include the

United States Virgin Islands, purchased from the Dutch in 1917, and American Samoa, acquired in an 1899 treaty with Germany that divided the Samoan archipelago.

The Consequences of Manifest Destiny

There is no doubt that the doctrine of Manifest Destiny made the United States a richer, more powerful nation. In addition to the wealth of land and natural resources that were gained, the nation's territorial expansion, which coincided with the Industrial Revolution, resulted in unprecedented growth and prosperity. The technological innovations derived from the confluence of these two forces allowed the United States to become the global superpower that it is today. Moreover, the United States' spread across the North American continent meant the removal of European powers from the land and, consequently, significantly reduced the threat of foreign interference in American interests.

However, Manifest Destiny came with its share of atrocities. In addition to the Mexican-American War, the decimation of the Native American population and the United States Civil War are most notable.

Impact on Native Americans

American expansion spelled doom for Native Americans. As white explorers, fur trappers, missionaries, and settlers moved westward, Native Americans lost their possessions and then their lives. In general, Americans regarded the indigenous population as a threat to the progression of the "civilized" American way of life. It was a threat that had to be removed.

The Northwest Ordinance of 1787 promised that Indian lands would not be invaded or taken except "in just wars authorized by

During his annual message to Congress on December 6, 1830, President Andrew Jackson addressed the issue of Indian removal to lands west of the Mississippi River. By this time, a number of Indian tribes had agreed to relocate. Jackson saw this development as an inducement to other tribes to do so as well. Nevertheless, thousands of Indians died while being forcefully removed from their homes. Refer to page 57 for a partial transcription.

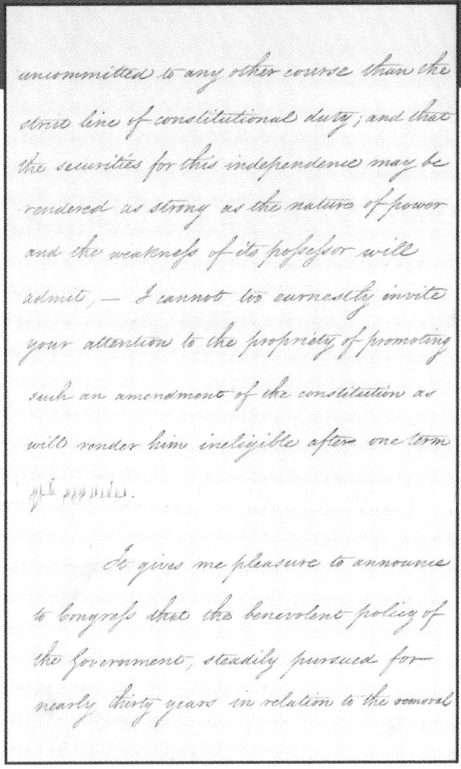
uncommitted to any other course than the strict line of constitutional duty; and that the securities for this independence may be rendered as strong as the nature of power and the weakness of its possessor will admit, — I cannot too earnestly invite your attention to the propriety of promoting such an amendment of the constitution as will render him ineligible after one term of service.

It gives me pleasure to announce to Congress that the benevolent policy of the Government, steadily pursued for nearly thirty years in relation to the removal

Congress," and the Constitution gave Congress the power to regulate commerce with "the Indian tribes." Nevertheless, Native Americans had virtually no rights in expansionist America.

In 1823, the U.S. Supreme Court ruled in the case of *Johnson v. McIntosh* that the American Indians had no right to their land. Writing for the Court, Chief Justice John Marshall said that the American Indians were "wanderers of the Earth." They therefore ceded their rights to European and Anglo-American settlers. They were allowed to occupy the land, though they could not own it in the same way the new settlers could. The ruling was immediately used as a justification to kick the American Indians off their land.

In 1830, Congress passed the Indian Removal Act of 1830. It gave the president the authority to buy Indian homelands in the East in exchange for lands west of the Mississippi. A number of tribes unsuccessfully challenged the law in the Supreme Court and mounted other forms of resistance. Nevertheless, they were driven off their homeland in a forced march that became known as the Trail of Tears, during which up to 8,000 people died.

The *Johnson v. McIntosh* ruling and the Indian Removal Act of 1830 set precedents for dealing with the Native Americans that settlers encountered as the United States acquired additional territories. American law had made Native Americans dependents of the United States government but had guaranteed them little protection and no liberties. Between 1776 and 1900, the Native American population dwindled from more than 10 million to approximately 250,000 people. Those who survived were forced to live on desert reservations or other allotted lands, where they were expected to abandon their way of life and become more Americanized.

The American Civil War

The expansion of the United States during the early to middle nineteenth century intensified a long-running quarrel over slavery between pro-slavery states in the South and antislavery states in the North. The quarrel can be traced back to the drafting of the United States Constitution. Many of the states wanted to abolish slavery. In response, influential Southern slaveholders threatened to withdraw from the Union. In the interest of getting all the states to approve the Constitution, the nation's founders made a number of compromises regarding slavery. Each state was allowed to decide for itself on the legality of slavery. Also, the founders agreed on a formula for taking into account a state's slave population in determining the size of its congressional delegation. They set up a fugitive slave law to allow slave owners to reclaim runaway slaves. In addition, they outlawed the importation and exportation of slaves.

However, the Constitution did not anticipate the territorial expansion of the country. Therefore, it had no provisions on the legality of slavery in newly acquired territories or the new states that eventually were incorporated from those territories. As the United States gained more land, the North and South jostled over whether slavery should be allowed there. Between 1818 and 1854, three major compromises were reached in Congress to maintain a balance in the number of free states and slave states. The Missouri Compromise of 1820 was reached after Missouri applied for statehood as a slave state. The Compromise of 1850 dealt with the demands of free and slave states concerning all the territories acquired from Mexico after the Mexican-American War. The Kansas-Nebraska Act of 1854 left the question of legality of slavery in the Kansas and Nebraska territories, as they applied for statehood, to the settlers of those territories.

The quarrel between the two regions reached a boiling point with the election of antislavery Abraham Lincoln as president. Lincoln was opposed to slavery spreading to new territories. His election led more influential Southern slaveholders to conclude that withdrawing from the Union was the only way to guarantee their economic interests and rights to slavery. Within months after the election, thirteen Southern states seceded (withdrew) from the Union and formed the Confederate States of America. On April 12, 1861, a little more than a month after Lincoln's inauguration as president, Confederate forces opened fire on a Union fort in South Carolina. This act started the Civil War, during which approximately 618,000 Americans lost their lives.

Manifest Destiny Today

Although the era of Manifest Destiny has long been ended, its influence could be felt on every American foreign policy decision throughout the twentieth century. Manifest Destiny could

This map of the United States was created in 1857, four years before the Civil War. It shows the extent of slaveholding states and territories (denoted in red) and free states and territories (shown in green). As the United States acquired new territories, politicians from the North and the South engaged in bitter debates over whether slavery should be allowed in them.

be heard in President John F. Kennedy's plan to put a man on the moon before 1970. Moreover, it echoes in the United States' foreign policies that justify American forays into dozens of other countries. The notion that America has a duty to spread democracy around the world may be as common today as was the idea of America's right to expand during the nineteenth century. Manifest Destiny looms large in the United States' national character.

PRIMARY SOURCE TRANSCRIPTIONS

Page 9: Northwest Ordinance (Excerpt)

TRANSCRIPTION

An Ordinance for the government of the Territory of the United States northwest of the River Ohio.

Section 1. Be it ordained by the United States in Congress assembled, That the said territory, for the purposes of temporary government, be one district, subject, however, to be divided into two districts, as future circumstances may, in the opinion of Congress, make it expedient . . .

Sec. 9. So soon as there shall be five thousand free male inhabitants of full age in the district, upon giving proof thereof to the governor, they shall receive authority, with time and place, to elect a representative from their counties or townships to represent them in the general assembly. . .

Sec. 13. And, for extending the fundamental principles of civil and religious liberty, which form the basis whereon these republics, their laws and constitutions are erected; to fix and establish those principles as the basis of all laws, constitutions, and governments, which forever hereafter shall be formed in the said territory: to provide also for the establishment of States, and permanent government therein, and for their admission to a share in the federal councils on an equal footing with the original States, at as early periods as may be consistent with the general interest . . .

Art. 6. There shall be neither slavery nor involuntary servitude in the said territory, otherwise than in the punishment of crimes whereof the party shall have been duly convicted: Provided, always, That any person escaping into the same, from whom labor or service is lawfully claimed in any one of the original States, such fugitive may be lawfully reclaimed and conveyed to the person claiming his or her labor or service as aforesaid.

Page 20: The Texas Declaration of Independence (Excerpt)

TRANSCRIPTION

The Unanimous Declaration of Independence made by the Delegates of the People of Texas in General Convention at the town of Washington on the 2nd day of March 1836.
When a government has ceased to protect the lives, liberty and property of the people, from whom its legitimate powers are derived, and for the advancement of whose happiness it was instituted, and so far from being a guarantee for the enjoyment of those inestimable and inalienable rights, becomes an instrument in the hands of evil rulers for their oppression. . .

When, in consequence of such acts of malfeasance and abdication on the part of the government, anarchy prevails, and civil society is dissolved into its original elements. In such a crisis, the first law of nature, the right of self-preservation, the inherent and inalienable rights of the people to appeal to first principles, and take their political affairs into their own hands in extreme cases, enjoins it as a right towards themselves, and a sacred obligation to their posterity, to abolish such government, and create another in its stead, calculated to rescue them from impending dangers, and to secure their future welfare and happiness. . .

These, and other grievances, were patiently borne by the people of Texas, until they reached that point at which forbearance ceases to be a virtue. We then took up arms in defence of the national constitution. We appealed to our Mexican brethren for assistance. Our appeal has been made in vain. Though months have elapsed, no sympathetic response has yet been heard from the Interior. We are, therefore, forced to the melancholy conclusion, that the Mexican people have acquiesced in the destruction of their liberty, and the substitution therfor of a military government; that they are unfit to be free, and incapable of self government.

The necessity of self-preservation, therefore, now decrees our eternal political separation.

We, therefore, the delegates with plenary powers of the people of Texas, in solemn convention assembled, appealing to a candid world for the necessities of our condition, do hereby resolve and declare, that our political connection with the Mexican nation has forever ended, and that the people of Texas do now constitute a free, Sovereign, and independent republic, and are fully invested with all the rights and attributes which properly belong to independent nations; and, conscious of the rectitude of our intentions, we fearlessly and confidently commit the issue to the decision of the Supreme arbiter of the destinies of nations.

Page 29: Oregon Treaty of 1846 (Excerpt)

TRANSCRIPTION

Treaty with Great Britain, in Regard to Limits Westward of the Rocky Mountains.

THE United States of America and her Majesty the Queen of the United Kingdom of Great Britain and Ireland, deeming it to be desirable for the future welfare of both countries that the state of doubt and uncertainty which has hitherto prevailed respecting the sovereignty and government of the territory on the northwest coast of America, lying westward of the Rocky or Stony Mountains, should be finally terminated by an amicable compromise of the rights mutually asserted by the two parties over the said territory, have respectively named plenipotentiaries to treat and agree concerning the terms of such settlement—that is to say: the President of the United States of America has, on his part, furnished with full powers James Buchanan, Secretary of State of the United States, and her Majesty the Queen of the United Kingdom of Great Britain and Ireland has, on her part, appointed the Right Honorable Richard Pakenham, a member of her Majesty's Most Honorable Privy Council, and her Majesty's Envoy Extraordinary and Minister Plenipotentiary to the United States; who, after having communicated to each other their respective full powers, found in good and due form, have agreed upon and concluded the following articles:—

ARTICLE I.

From the point on the forty-ninth parallel of north latitude, where the boundary laid down in existing treaties and conventions between the United States and Great Britain terminates, the line of boundary between the territories of the United States and those of her Britannic Majesty shall be continued westward along the said forty-ninth parallel of north latitude to the middle of the channel which separates the continent from Vancouver's Island, and thence southerly through the middle of the said channel, and of Fuca's Straits, to the Pacific Ocean: Provided, however, That the navigation of the whole of the said channel and straits, south of the forty-ninth parallel of north latitude, remain free and open to both parties.

JAMES BUCHANAN [L S.]
RICHARD PAKENHAM [L. S.]

Page 43: Treaty of Guadalupe Hidalgo (Excerpt)

TRANSCRIPTION

IN THE NAME OF ALMIGHTY GOD

The United States of America and the United Mexican States animated by a sincere desire to put an end to the calamities of the war which unhappily exists between the two Republics and to establish Upon a solid basis relations of peace and friendship, which shall confer reciprocal benefits upon the citizens of both, and assure the concord, harmony, and mutual confidence wherein the two people should live, as good neighbors have for that purpose appointed their respective plenipotentiaries, that is to say: The President of the United States has appointed Nicholas P. Trist, a citizen of the United States, and the President of the Mexican Republic has appointed Don Luis Gonzaga Cuevas, Don Bernardo Couto, and Don Miguel Atristain, citizens of the said Republic; Who, after a reciprocal communication of their respective full powers, have, under the protection of Almighty God, the author of peace, arranged, agreed upon, and signed the following: Treaty of Peace, Friendship, Limits, and Settlement between the United States of America and the Mexican Republic.

ARTICLE I

There shall be firm and universal peace between the United States of America and the Mexican Republic, and between their respective countries, territories, cities, towns, and people, without exception of places or persons . . .

ARTICLE XII

In consideration of the extension acquired by the boundaries of the United States, as defined in the fifth article of the present treaty, the Government of the United States engages to pay to that of the Mexican Republic the sum of fifteen millions of dollars.

Page 51: Excerpt from "On Indian Removal," President Andrew Jackson's address to Congress on December 6, 1830

TRANSCRIPTION

It gives me pleasure to announce to Congress that the benevolent policy of the Government, steadily pursued for nearly thirty years, in relation to the removal of the Indians beyond the white settlements is approaching to a happy consummation. Two important tribes have accepted the provision made for their removal at the last session of Congress, and it is believed that their example will induce the remaining tribes also to seek the same obvious advantages.

The consequences of a speedy removal will be important to the United States, to individual States, and to the Indians themselves. The pecuniary advantages which it promises to the Government are the least of its recommendations. It puts an end to all possible danger of collision between the authorities of the General and State Governments on account of the Indians. It will place a dense and civilized population in large tracts of country now occupied by a few savage hunters. By opening the whole territory between Tennessee on the north and Louisiana on the south to the settlement of the whites it will incalculably strengthen the southwestern frontier and render the adjacent States strong enough to repel future invasions without remote aid. It will relieve the whole State of Mississippi and the western part of Alabama of Indian occupancy, and enable those States to advance rapidly in population, wealth, and power. It will separate the Indians from immediate contact with settlements of whites; free them from the power of the States; enable them to pursue happiness in their own way and under their own rude institutions; will retard the progress of decay, which is lessening their numbers, and perhaps cause them gradually, under the protection of the Government and through the influence of good counsels, to cast off their savage habits and become an interesting, civilized, and Christian community.

GLOSSARY

Anglo-American   An American of European descent.

annexation   The act of making a smaller territory part of a larger nation.

boomtown   A town that rapidly grows in size due to a new industry.

cede   To surrender property to a larger entity.

colonialism   The policy of a larger country taking control of a smaller country for financial benefit.

depose   To remove a leader from power.

expansionism   The belief in increasing the size of one's national territory.

Industrial Revolution   The period of rapid technological change and development in the eighteenth and nineteenth centuries, during which many Western nations were transformed from agricultural societies to ones with economies based on factories and mechanization.

insurgent   A person who rebels against authority.

mission system   A system of churches and outposts in a foreign country designed to convert the country's native people to Christianity.

nationalism   A strong belief in one's country.

nomad   A person who travels from place to place, without a fixed home.

secular   Not religious in nature.

utopia   An ideal social or political system.

FOR MORE INFORMATION

California Historical Society
678 Mission Street
San Francisco, CA 94105
(415) 357-1848
Web site: http://www.californiahistoricalsociety.org

The Texas Historical Commission
1511 Colorado
Austin, TX 78701
(512) 463-6100
e-mail: thc@thc.state.tx.us
Web site: http://www.thc.state.tx.us

Web Sites

Due to the changing nature of Internet links, the Rosen Publishing
Group, Inc., has developed an online list of Web sites related to the
subject of this book. This site is updated regularly. Please use this link
to access the list:

http://www.rosenlinks.com/psah/made

# FOR FURTHER READING

Merk, Frederick. *Manifest Destiny and Mission in American History.* New York: Vintage Books, 1966.

Mills, Bronwyn. *The Mexican War* (America at War). New York: Facts On File, 1992.

Zinn, Howard. *A People's History of the United States: 1492–Present.* New York: Perennial, 2003.

# BIBLIOGRAPHY

Beckham, Stephen Dow. "Oregon History." Retrieved August 27, 2003 (http://bluebook.state.or.us/cultural/history/history.htm).

Bowen, Catherine Drinker. *Miracle at Philadelphia: The Story of the Constitutional Convention, May to September, 1787.* Boston: Back Bay Books, 1966.

California History Online. Retrieved August 28, 2003 (http://www.californiahistory.net).

Everything2.com. "Manifest Destiny." Retrieved August 19, 2003 (http://www.everything2.com/index.pl?node=Manifest%20Destiny).

Everything2.com. "Philippines." Retrieved August 29, 2003 (http://www.everything2.com/index.pl?node_id=22521).

Everything2.com. "Texas." Retrieved August 20, 2003 (http://www. everything2.com/index.pl?node=Texas).

Hawaii State Government. "A Brief History of Hawaii." Retrieved August 29, 2003 (http://www.state.hi.us/about/history.htm).

Hietala, Thomas. *Manifest Design: Anxious Aggrandizement in Late Jacksonian America.* Ithaca, NY: Cornell University Press, 1985.

Merk, Frederick. *Manifest Destiny and Mission in American History.* New York: Vintage Books, 1966.

Mills, Bronwyn. *The Mexican War* (America at War). New York: Facts On File, 1992.

Zinn, Howard. *A People's History of the United States: 1492–Present.* New York: Perennial, 2003.

PRIMARY SOURCE IMAGE LIST

Page 9: Page from the Northwest Ordinance, July 13, 1787. Housed at the National Archives in Washington, D.C.

Page 11: Portrait of Thomas Jefferson, oil on panel, 1805, by Gilbert Stuart. Housed at the National Portrait Gallery, Smithsonian Institution in Washington, D.C.

Page 12: Map of North America, 1803, by John Luffman. Housed at the Library of Congress Geography and Map Division in Washington, D.C.

Page 14: Portrait of James Madison, engraving by David Edwin after an original by Thomas Sully. Housed at the Library of Congress Prints and Photographs Division in Washington, D.C.

Page 17: Map of the Province of Texas, 1822, by Stephen F. Austin.

Page 20: Texas Declaration of Independence, 1836. Housed at the Texas State Library & Archives Commission.

Page 26: *Astoria*, engraving by Avery after Parsons, 1836.

Page 28: Portrait of President James Polk, lithograph by Currier & Ives, created between 1840 and 1849. Housed at the Library of Congress Prints and Photographs Division in Washington, D.C.

Page 29: Oregon Treaty, August 5, 1846. Housed at the National Archives and Records Administration in Washington, D.C.

Page 35: Portrait of John Charles Fremont, undated hand-colored lithograph. Courtesy of Bancroft Library, University of California, Berkeley.

Page 37: Portrait of Antonio López de Santa Anna, oil on linen, by Paul L'Ouvrier, 1858. Housed at the New-York Historical Society.

Page 40 (top): Portrait of Major General Winfield Scott, color lithograph by Currier & Ives, 1847. Housed at the Library of Congress Prints and Photographs Division in Washington, D.C.

Page 40 (bottom): *Battle of Buena Vista*, color lithograph by Currier & Ives, circa 1847. Housed at the Library of Congress Prints and Photographs Division in Washington, D.C.

Page 43: Treaty of Guadalupe Hidalgo, 1848. Housed at the National Archives and Records Administration in Washington, D.C.

Page 47: Check for the purchase of Alaska, 1868. Housed at the National Archives and Records Administration in Washington, D.C.

Page 48: Illustration of King Kamehameha I of Hawaii, circa 1820.

Page 51: President Andrew Jackson's message to Congress "On Indian Removal," December 6, 1830. Housed at the National Archives and Records Administration in Washington, D.C.

Page 54: Map of the United States, 1857, engraved by W. & A. K. Johnston. Housed at the Library of Congress Geography and Map Division in Washington, D.C.

NDEX

About the Author

J.T. Moriarty is a freelance writer who lives in Brooklyn, New York. He has written for *Oberlin Review* and made contributions to the Center for Anthropological Computing's literary journal.

Photo Credits

Cover, pp. 14, 28, 40 (top and bottom) Library of Congress, Prints and Photographs Division; pp. 1, 26, 30 © Hulton Archive/Getty Images; p. 9 National Archives and Records Administration, Records of the Continental and Confederation Congresses and the Constitutional Convention, 1774-1789, Record Group 360; p. 11 National Portrait Gallery, Smithsonian Institution, gift of the Regents of the Smithsonian Institution, the Thomas Jefferson Memorial Foundation, and the Enid and Crosby Kemper Foundation, owned jointly with Monticello; pp. 12, 54 Library of Congress, Geography and Map Division; p. 17 © Corbis; pp. 19, 20 courtesy Texas State Library and Archives Commission; pp. 22, 33, 48 © Bettmann/Corbis; pp. 29, 43 National Archives and Records Administration, General Records of the United States Government, 1778-1992, Record Group 11; pp. 32, 35 courtesy of the Bancroft Library, University of California, Berkeley; p. 37 © New-York Historical Society/Bridgeman Art Library; p. 47 National Archives and Records Administration, Records of the Accounting Officers of the Department of the Treasury, Record Group 217; p. 51 President Jackson's Message to Congress "On Indian Removal", December 6, 1830; Records of the United States Senate, 1789-1990; Record Group 46; Records of the United States Senate, 1789-1990; National Archive.

Designer: Nelson Sà; **Editor:** Wayne Anderson; **Photo Researcher:** Peter Tomlinson